Empower

Publishing

Watch for More Titles
by Annette Martin Collins

from *Empower Publishing*

Ponderings
of a Lifetime

Poetry, Memories &
Wisdom

by

Annette Martin Collins

Empower Publishing
Winston-Salem
2020

Empower

Publishing

Empower Publishing
PO Box 26701
Winston-Salem, NC 27114

First Empower Publishing Books edition published
May, 2020
Empower Publishing, Feather Pen and all production design are trademarks.

For information regarding bulk purchases of this book, digital purchase and special discounts, please contact the publisher at empowerpublishing2015@gmail.com

Cover design by Pan Morelli
Cover image: Annette, Shelly, Gerry & Emily, 1969

Manufactured in the United States of America
ISBN 978-1-63066-506-7

Dedication

It is with pride and gratefulness that I dedicate the pages within this book to four strong women. Patricia Anne Collins, daughter, who is a registered nurse. Michele Elaine Collins, a retired truck driver. In memory of Emily Beaudry Martin, my mother, and Rose Simpson Collins, my dear mother-in-law.

The love and encouragement I received from these four women allowed me to live my best life. It has been an unforgettable journey.

This book has been brought about due to the threat of Covid-19. I am now in my eighties and not in the best of health. Just in case the Corona Virus knocks at my door, I want to leave something behind for my family. My cherished possessions are few. A roll-top desk, a big brown comfy chair, and an old KIA.

What could I leave behind? I thought to gather a few stories and poems written over the past fifty years and put them into a book of memories. If I wait, they will disappear, as I have memory issues.

I hope that you enjoy the poems and short stories.

Respectfully,

—Annette Martin Collins

Acknowledgements

About the people to whom I dedicated this book:

Dear readers,

Since I am new to putting together writings from over the past fifty years, I would like to tell you a little about myself. I live with my two daughters in Winston-Salem, NC. We live in an old 'fixer-upper' house and for the past twenty years there have been continuous projects happening within these walls and on the grounds.

First, let me tell you about my daughter, Patty. I look up to her as someone I could have been had I made better choices in my early life. Her professors in college thought she should go to law school, but she chose a nursing career. People enjoy being around Patty as she is always upbeat, joyful and witty, Patty takes a nap, then gets up and tells us about the new project she has thought of, and then how to do it.

Shelly, my second daughter, worked as a truck driver for the last twenty years. I would follow her to the ends of the earth, as there is nothing Shelly cannot do. If there is something that needs fixing, or to be built, Shelly can figure it out.

Next would be my mother, Emily. She died in Florida after eighteen years of Alzheimer's disease at age eighty-nine. I was her only child. Emily left school after the fifth grade to work as a housekeeper until she was twelve, then went to work in a thread mill. Mother was an alcoholic, perhaps hereditary, as my grandfather, too, was an alcoholic. But mother worked all her life, and was an excellent housekeeper and cook. She was, to me, the most beautiful lady and elegant in stature. I did fear her when she drank. This was in my youth, and perhaps she was unhappy in marriage. She only drank at home, and she would fight with my father, but he would never fight back. He would go down to the cellar and work on his amateur radio equipment. He would talk to people all over the world in code. When mother was in one of her moods, I would join him in the basement. As I recall, it was only every other weekend.

Now for Rose, my mother-in-law. I was seventeen when I met her son. I was head over heels in love with this guy. The first boyfriend I ever had, and wouldn't you know it, I got pregnant. Patty and I graduated high school to together in June of 1956. I got married in September. For the next twenty-four years it was a one-sided marriage. I loved him, but he never loved me back. He showed me no respect, but there was someone who did love me. It was Rose, my mother-in-law. She was so good to me. I felt that I was getting one over on my husband. I stole his mother from him!

—AMC

Contents

My Truth

My truth is, I chose a writing class to become motivated to write my story. Everyone has a story to tell. Did you know that my great grandmother, an Indian, was the lone survivor of a massacre between the French and Indians in the 1800's in northern Canada. She was adopted by a Catholic family from Boston, MA. She married an artist who painted pictures on ceilings in churches. He died of lead poisoning at a young age.

My grandmother, Anna, married Felix Beaudry. He had auburn hair and green eyes and I know this as I saw pictures of them. Felix worked on the railroad, and Anna ran a boarding house in their home. They had five children all of whom were sent out to work by the age of ten. Most, working in the local thread mill. Felix was an alcoholic and would stop at the pub each night, then go home and beat up my grandmother. The girls would hide their mother so he could not find her. Felix died at a fairly young age of a heart attack, or so they say. Mother told me her mother could have given him something to cause the heart attack. Who knows?

My dad was eleven years older than mother. She was twenty-six when they married. Father was a tool and die maker. He built a ham radio station from scratch in our basement and every night he would come home from work and after supper retreat to the basement to spend hours talking to people all over the world in Morse code. He also loved to fish and hunt.

Mother always worked. I can never remember a time when she did not work. She was an involved mother, always pushing me into music and dance. A really good cook, an excellent housekeeper, all the things one would want in a mother. She had one flaw. She had alcoholic tendencies. Twice a month she would bring home a bottle and two weekends a month she would drink and get mean. Perhaps it was hereditary. Her father was mean when he drank. When these bad days occurred, I always asked my dad to take me with him when he went fishing, or I would stay down in the basement while he played on his radio. Mother was the perfect lady at all times, except when she drank.

At seventeen, with the first boyfriend I ever had, I became pregnant. When I told him that I was pregnant he punched a big dent into the dash of his car. This was June. We married in September. I had three children by age twenty. He was an abusive alcoholic. Our marriage lasted 24 years. I had jumped from the frying pan into the fire!

Emily Beaudry, Age 20

The Perfect Rose

How many petals form a rose
Mused I while loading my pallet
The background must be of the softest hue
For one perfect flower and a chalice.
*

Unaware of time was I
As hours slipped into history
Melancholy consumed my mind
I could not escape its mystery.
*

Pure colors kissed and blended
In quiet harmony
Across the waiting canvas
Well… almost reverently
*

I'll need silver for the chalice
With perhaps a fleck of gold
Angel white the petals
And a stem of green quite bold
*

A splash of tears was the autograph
This painting was like no other
For gazing up from the canvas at me
Was the youthful face of my mother.

Annette Martin Collins

Where the Lilacs Bloom

Where the lilac's bloom
Outside grandma's kitchen
That's where we sat
Eating cookies on the step.
Where the lilac's bloom
Outside grandma's kitchen
That's where we stood
For pictures after graduation
Where the lilac's bloom
Outside grandma's kitchen
That's where we would congregate
For our family reunions
Whistling through broken panes
The wind calls to grandma
But she is gone
(or is she)
Where the lilac's bloom

It's March…Enough Already!

It felt like sleet, it looked like snow
Two days and nights the wind did blow
The power is out and the phones are dead
Can't get to work, go back to bed.
Snug in their nest the hen's eggs froze
The geese and the ducks together dozed
The deer in the woods lay silent and still
The coyotes are howling
Echo's heard from the hills
The rabbits wild beneath the barn stayed
The hungry fox from his den strayed.
Through every crack the bitter winds whip
Cats under wood stove their sleek fur lick.
Beneath heavy branches evergreens bow low
Until SNAP, CRACK, to the ground they go.
To keep out the cold more wood for the stove
While angry thoughts of winter I drove.
Sleet driven rain onto windows it pummeled
Leaks on the porch into pails were funneled.
Now covering the ice comes more and more snow
It laces the panes as the north winds blow
Words which I spoke, remembering well
Me…like the snow? A cold day in hell!
The sun has appeared in a sky of grey
A crystal world before me lay.
For after all is said and done how can I criticize
For peering out the window pane, Earth's beauty hypnotizes.

Nine-Eleven

Nine-Eleven. How could anyone forget this date. I was at work in Cocoa, Florida. The company was Community Services Council, and I was their secretary/receptionist/accounting clerk. I worked for the president and also the comptroller. We were a good team and I loved my job. I lived in nearby Merritt Island, about a ten-minute drive across the Indian River. We were all getting starting in our day's work when Bill called for us to gather in his office. There was a TV in his office, and sadly we watched as one plane after another crashed into the twin towers. There were no dry eyes in the whole building. Everyone went home. No one could work after seeing that!

For the next three days I thought about life and how fragile it is. One of my daughters lived in Cocoa, but she was married and had her own home. She was doing OK, but my other daughter was in nursing school in Maine and she lived alone, off campus. She was going to graduate from the University of Maine with a BSN in nursing at the end of December. After talking to her on the phone, I gave a three-month notice at work, and in December I packed up what was left in my condo and drove to Maine.

There was a heavy cloud of thick sediment remaining over the city of New York as I drove past. Heavy air, heavy heart, heavy thoughts.

I hate driving at night. I hate driving in the rain. I hate driving on the interstate highways. I was excited about returning to Maine, but I was in a terrible mood. It was raining heavily. Trucks were whizzing past me on both sides splashing water on both sides of me plus on my windshield. Not bad enough, they had to blast their air-horns as they went by. Some even gestured with sign language, but I do not know sign language, so I just mimicked what they did to me.

This has to end. The rain did not let up, nor did the traffic. The speed limit was 65 MPH. I never drive over 60 normally, however, when it rains, and when it is dark, I have a hard time laying on the gas pedal to reach 45-mph. My feet just won't do it. Besides I could not even see the lane I was in. I am the trucker's worse nightmare.

Well, enough of this! My best friend (and co-pilot) had been complaining about everything. Trying to get my attention to get off the road. I finally listened to him and found a motel off Interstate 95 north of Boston. We had stopped for the night. I know he was burned out from all his yelling at me. I don't think he will ever want to do another road trip with me.

We went to bed and snuggled until we both fell asleep. His name is Rascal. He's my cat.

New York City

My daughter Patty was coming from Maine to Connecticut for a visit. Daughter Shelly had two children and they were at an age where they could enjoy a train ride into New York City. I had Emily. I packed an extra set of clothing for Emily in case she had to go to the bathroom and I did not get her to the toilet in time. Emily enjoyed walking and simply being where the action was. She loved little children and always offered them a nickel, dime or quarter when we were out shopping. What could go wrong?

The train ride was fun. We watched people getting on and off at the scheduled stops. We got off at Grand Central Station and proceeded to walk around the grand city, mostly window shopping. We had lunch in a cafeteria, then went to Macy's. There were so many people in the store isles that it must have been confusing to Emily.

I took my eyes off her for what seemed like only a minute and she was gone. The girls and I looked up and down the isles, as did the boys. Ezekiel spotted her first. "There she is Gram!" he called out.

Oh, my! There stood Emily, holding up a pair of her nice clean bloomers and offering them to a little boy in a stroller. The kid was screaming!

I was glad to get home that night. It was a LONG day.

I Am Who I Am (at 76)

I sit at my computer this morning remembering my mother and father. There are so many questions I wish I had asked when they were alive. It is too late now. I currently live with my two daughters, and I have a son whom I see occasionally. No one ever asks questions. AHA! That's it! I will write about who I am at this very moment in time. GOD Himself can ask me the questions and I will have to answer truthfully as no one can lie to GOD! So… here goes!

GOD: Good morning, and just for the record, what is your name?

ANNETTE: Annette Marie Martin Collins

GOD: How are you today?

ANNETTE: I am well, thank you. Feeling no pain from arthritis and I had a good night's sleep. I am happy.

GOD: Have you had a good life thus far?

ANNETTE: Yes. Of course, there have been some rough times, but the good outweighs the bad. I thank you for my three children. They are a blessing. They endured my past and know how it was. Can we please not talk about the past?

GOD: OK then. Let's concentrate on the present. Oh, by the way, the present is my gift to you.

ANNETTE: Yes, I know, and I thank you every day for the present.

GOD: So what is going on with you now?

ANNETTE: Well, I attend the Covenant Presbyterian Church USA. Write the newsletter monthly for them. The church sign out in front of the church is one of my responsibilities. The saying gets changed once a week and I try to put up good messages to bring people in to visit. So far it is not working. I will keep trying. That is what brought me into this little church, the sign out front.

GOD: So, you are a Presbyterian?

ANNETTE: Right now I am. I was a cradle Catholic for my first forty years. Then I left that church and joined the Unitarian Universalist church. From there I visited many other denominations, joined a Southern Baptist Church while I was in Florida. Once I moved back to North Carolina, this charming little church around the corner from where I live drew me in with the sign out front and I've been hooked ever since. I found them to be good people and the people are the church, right?

GOD: Yes, the people are the church. Are you happy there?

ANNETTE: I am. I am presently a ruling elder, have responsibilities, am a Session Member. I belong to the Women's Circle that meets once a month. This gives me purpose. I could be at home every day watching TV and feeling lonely. Both girls are work-a-holics, so I am alone a lot at home. I need to feel useful. I crochet hats for cancer patients, and make shawls and afghans for giving away. I started a prayer shawl ministry at church but it seems I am the only member. If we could grow our church perhaps there would be others that would like to join me. We are down to only about thirty members. Most are in their seventies and eighties. I guess at this age they have have pretty much run out of steam.

GOD: Keep on trying. It is in freely giving that you receive.

ANNETTE: I have always felt close to you. Does it really matter what denomination a person is? I found good people in every church I attended. They all love you. I believe that you are always with me. It is a good feeling.

GOD: Denominations are made by man, along with rules. Have you read my book? In it I promised to be with you always. I did not say I would be with only the Presbyterians, the Catholics, or the Methodists. I am with you (all of you) always. Do you realize that when you are practicing hospitality, you are entertaining ME as well? When you look into the eyes of a stranger you are seeing ME and I am seeing you. I created mankind in my own image.

ANNETTE: WOW! What an awesome thought. I see you every day and was not aware of it. You are in every one of your creations. Are you in the birds and animals, the trees, mountains and rivers?

GOD: I am in all of my creation. All of creation is connected. When terror strikes and multitudes die, I am there.

Evil exists in the world due to free will. Some chose to worship power, greed, money, but all will die and their spoils will remain here. I am there to welcome my children home.

ANNETTE: Thank you for all of your creation. Oh, and thank you for allowing me to be here this long. Love my life now, better than ever. I have never traveled much so most of your Earth I have not seen with my own eyes. Just on TV sometimes. I am hoping that when I die, I can travel around the world and see all the places I've wondered about. Is this possible? Yes or no?

GOD: If you can think it, you can do it. You could do it now, but your faith is not strong enough. There are many things you can do now. One of your gifts is creativity. Some folks sing, some play instruments, some write stories, some build things. There are many that spend their whole lives helping others to have better lives. Teachers would be a good example of this.

ANNETTE: When I die, will I come back?

GOD: If that is what you want to do. Most people choose to become a part of who I AM. They cling on to the whole, which is GOD, and enjoy all the peace, love, and rest. This can last forever, or at some point, you can choose to live again and try to do better at life than your prior times. You just need to let go and *become* again.

ANNETTE: Oh, this thought gives me so much peace. I can choose my own destiny. This is not Presbyterian teaching. But as you said before, denominations are man-made. It is good to believe in YOU and pray for one another. You have sent your very own SON to point the way to YOU. Thank you for that.

GOD: You're welcome. I did send my son, JESUS, and he is the perfect example of how a human being should live. There have been many other people with messages through the ages, and there are even more today. They are all basically exclaiming the same thing. Love one another as I have loved you. Share the Earth. Feed the hungry. Care for the sick. I have provided for all your needs.

A Summer of Reflection

My year began by getting to know my son, Gerry, again after a decade of living in upstate New York. He came to North Carolina after he lost his right leg and then his wife died. He wanted to begin a new life. I wanted to help him. I know Gerry had a problem with drugs and alcohol. I did not realize how bad it had gotten. On February 8th, at the age of 57 and three months, he died.

My spring and summer were consumed with sole searching and trying to put all the pieces of a fractured life together and discover my own truths. This has been extremely painful for me. I discovered there are two personalities residing within me.

Annette was an only child with all the advantages. Brought up in a home with two parents who worked and attended church every Sunday. We did everything as a family and life was good. My father never drank and he was a tool and die maker who worked for an engineering firm. My mother worked in an aircraft factory. She kept a spotless house, and her cooking was wonderful. She was also an alcoholic. Thankfully she only drank on the weekend and only one or two weekends a month. She never drank outside the home. No one knew. When she drank, she became mean and I begged my father to take me fishing with him on Saturdays. By the time we returned, mother would be sleeping it off. Things became normal again.

Annie began making herself known in my sophomore year of high school. She was a funny, high spirited, wild, outgoing adventurist. She began to develop her own set of friends. Annette's friends and Annie's friends never met. In Annie's senior year of high-school she met Zeke Collins at a hot dog stand. His real name was Millard G. Collins. He was from the state of Maine. He drove a truck for a living and had a motorcycle. This was my first boyfriend and I fell head over heals for him. I suspected he had a drinking problem, but at seventeen, what did I know.

I told him that I was pregnant and that my mother said I could give up the baby, or she would raise the child and I could go to college. His reaction was terrifying to me. He slammed his fist into the dash of his car, causing a huge dent. He said that I should let HIM decide what HE wanted to do.

Well, we married. Twice. Annie married the devil himself by a Justice of the Peace. Annette had the marriage consecrated in the church. Our relationship went on the 24 years. I won't get into any details, but I can tell you that it was Annette who raised her three children. We four went to church. I was a Brownie Leader. We did all the things my parents provided me as a child. If I wanted to spend a Saturday night with my husband I had to go to his garage and drink with him and his friends. There were many of them. He was free with his money when it came to his friends. He developed his own trucking company and had a huge terminal in North Haven. Annie was a total cut-up around his friends. I guess I was always trying to impress him, or in competition with the floozies that the terminal attracted. His friends liked me. I will never know why he did not like me. I filed for divorce three times and on each occasion, he would come up with some fantastic gift and the promise to straighten up. The only blessing that I can see in my years with "Lucifer' is the truth that I loved his mother. She was so good to me and the children. Annie lived on during the duration of the marriage, but only occasionally. She would never cheat on her husband and he knew that. In fact, he would brag about it. All the while, he was notorious at being the sneak. They called him Zeke, the Sneak.

Millard, Annette & Patty

In defense of my poor choices during those 24-years, when Zeke came to the winter season of his life, another choice was made on his behalf. He had lost everything, and was in a shelter in Connecticut. Someone knocked him down and broke his shoulder. He was placed in a nursing home and we were called to advise us of his placement. My girls and I discussed the matter and decided they would drive to Connecticut and bring hm back to NC. We set him up in our front room. It was discovered he also had terminal lung cancer, so we got hospice involved. He had excellent care for his last year on earth. He was a horrid patient. Smoked non-stop, burning holes in blankets. Occasionally, he would light up five cigarettes at a time. He is now at peace.

Now, in defense of my breaking my own mother's heart by marrying at seventeen, when she turned 70 and could no longer live on her own, I took her in to live with me. For the next 18-years, I was at her side through the sad years of dementia. She died at age 88. My daughters and I did the same thing for my wonderful mother-in-law, Rose, with dementia for eight years. In Florida, we cared for Emily and Rose together for the last year of Emily's life.

My son followed the path of his father in alcoholism. His wife, Laura, was an alcoholic also. She died of a brain aneurism after Gerry lost his leg. They are both gone now. I miss Gerry. He had a good heart.

Gerry and Wife Laura in Vermont

Time

It isn't always easy being free
This person without roots
This person "ME"
Alone
Where is home?
I know not, yet I search
Time to me is a gift
Were this not so
I would be
fearful
So
moving on
This poor but
happy spirit travels
with the wind
adrift
When time
no more have I
To leave this shell
That I call
"ME"
No regrets be
For treasured friends
Long past, await
This is Eternity

Annette Martin Collins

Inheritance

Why do we measure wealth
In tangible possessions?
I know a person
Who has not a dime
But has to her credit
In eighty year's time
Silver hair
Emerald eyes
Ruby lips
Balm of cheerfulness
Her energy goes on and on
As freely of herself she gives
A smile, a touch, a comforting word
Keep safe this treasure while she lives
And when, alas, her life is spent
And when I, too, am eighty-three
May I inherit her treasured gifts
As daughter, and beneficiary

In Thanksgiving

What greater praise
Can we give to God
Than to be honest
Loving caretakers
Of this beautiful Earth.

Measuring Time

Darkness to light
Shadows, tides
Tree girth
Seasons
Human height
Spiritual growth

Insomnia

A metronome keeps time for me
As I create this poetry
It's hot tonight and I can't sleep
My thoughts are caught up in the beat
And things I really want to say
Crash forth like waves
Then slink away
The meter echo's like a clock
Tic…tick…tick…tock…tick…tick…tick…tock
To turn it off and go to bed
I can't, you see, it's in my head!

Fisherman's Luck

Fishing in Florida was on my bucket list. There are alligators, snakes, and in the salt water, sharks. The following short narration is a condensed version of my experience in February of 1989 in Golden Gate, Florida. First my friend and I fished south of Alligator Alley and then on to the west coast, just north of Naples.

While fishing in a small canal my line became quite stuck. Nervously I watched for snakes as I sank into the muck! Was that a log that I observed slip down the riverbank? My feet felt like they were in cement shoes. They made a sucking sound as I pulled them out of the water. I lost one sneaker. Could have been worse. I went in at 5 ft 7 in. Could have come out two feet shorter.

The following day I slowly waded across a channel to "Lover's Key". I stood in water to my waist while a school of mullet stared at me. No bites. No strikes, not even one. Looking back towards my blanket a family of raccoons were busy enjoying my lunch and then proceeded to haul off my Styrofoam cooler.

That evening I fished off a nearby bridge. There were many people fishing off this bridge. I felt a tug on my line and got so excited. As I looked into the water I saw a four-foot shadow with protruding fin swimming back and forth. He stole my catch, snapped my pole, ate my dinner.

A flock of birds flew over me while pouting on a bench, I sat. As I looked up, I knew (too late), I should have worn a HAT! I crossed out another item from my bucket list.

Summer Bounty

I picked a rose bouquet today
And placed it in a jar.
It sits upon my table now
The fragrance permeates afar.
So while it lasts I shall enjoy
The buds and petals white
Their loveliness for all to see
Especially me, oh my delight!
Alas, too soon the beauty fades
But throw them out… not me!
Into a covered tin I toss
My winter's store of potpourri.

The Witness

Standing in a dewy meadow
At the break of a new day
I observed a wreathe of mist
Floating earthward as if drawn
Towards the highest distant mountain
Of monumental girth.
God had slipped this ring of silver
On the hand of Mother Earth.

To My Sisters

I have reached my eightieth year. Here are a few things I would like to share with you that I have learned along my life's journey.

Oh, I could look back and wallow in my past and punish myself for all the misadventures that occurred. But why? I've lived through it all and survived. Every new day I start with a clean slate. I love my life and am so thankful for it.

Just look around at the person sitting next to you. She may be from another mother, but she is your sister, breathing the same air and living each day to its fullest. Some of us were from the 30's, 40's, 50's, 60's, 70's, 80's and later... but right at this moment we are all here together.

As I look around the table here, I want to tell you that I love you. I love to hear the stories that you share every month. When you are in pain I want to (fix it), but of course that is not possible. But know that I can feel it when you share.

When *you share* by telling of your adventures on planes, trains, and automobiles I am right there with you, experiencing all the senses as you recall them. I can feel the wind in my hair as I sit beside you on top of a train in a foreign country. I can see and smell the landscape in your stories, I feel the crush of people as I walk with you in a city in Africa.

Here is what I know. Every day, we start with a new clean slate. Every day I can make a contribution of one sort or another to make my world a better place, or I can waste my day by doing nothing.

I really don't care what religion you are, or how you worship, or not. We all follow our own belief system. I have been a Catholic, Baptist, Unitarian Universalist, and Presbyterian. I have wonderful friends in all of them.

Here is what I believe. I believe in creation. I believe there is One God, perhaps known by different names, but He is responsible for my being here at this exact time and place and I thank Him for my life. I thank Him for my children, my health, and my friends.

I know one day I will be gone. Like a daffodil that comes up in the spring, she returns to the earth when her time has expired. I believe in the promise of everlasting life. Our spirit lives on. What will it be like? In my mind, and unlike our world today, it will be void of hatred, pain, and greed. It will be a place of pure love.

Reminder: I love you, my sisters!

Shelly Drove for Werner

A Full House

The body cannot live
Without the soul
The soul cannot live
Without prayer
Prayer is conversation
Between mind and soul
To God…who is in us.

Doing Time

Sentenced to life on earth
Incarcerated in a body
The mind and the spirit debate
Time is all that you have
Time is all that you need
This is eternity
Time matters not

Pondering

Hypnotized by the wonders
Found 'round every turn
The wanderer slowly walks
Pondering

The Dreamer

In crafts, a fortune can be made
    she told me in the store.
I spent my whole week's pay and then
    I charged a wee bit more.
Flowers, eucalyptus, ribbons and bows,
    potpourri, candles and lace.
When I get a few more made,
    Upon each table a basket will grace.
As she checked out my purchases
    the shopkeeper slyly smiled
She knew, but unbeknownst to me,
    I would not be back for a while.
Rushing home with the lofty dreams
    as an entrepreneur, my goal.
I labored for hours, days and months
    with nary a basket sold.
In truth, a fortune can be made
    but not by me or you.
The shopkeeper drives a lovely new car.
    Mine's held together with glue!

The Cellophane Crystal Ball

My mother, Emily, worked for Pratt & Whitney in North Haven, CT and for the past two months she called me on the phone about this locally famous fortune-teller that her co-workers were talking about. Her name is Madam Bella. This lady is supposed to be the real deal, a true psychic, if there is such a thing. Mother calls every night telling me tales of tales, igniting the embers of my curious nature until it becomes a snapping, crackling blaze. Together we make the decision to call for an appointment. Our fate soon to be revealed from her lips to our ears.

It was cool and crisp that autumn day, October 13, 1979. This date sticks solidly in my mind mostly because it was a Friday, and I am superstitious. The leaves are falling from the trees and those that are left waved as I drove down South Cherry Street looking for house number seventy-two. I drove at a snail's pace. Turn back, turn back kept running through my head. I never listen. I could hear my heart beat. My preconception of the house was of a rundown, ram-shackled ominous dwelling with a broken gate. What I found was close. I must be psychic. A tall black iron fence enveloped the property as if to warn passersby of danger within. The gate was not broken.

Some things mother told me about this old woman were almost unbelievable. Twelve people once attended a party with Madam Bella as guest speaker. They all held hands and Madam Bella went one by one to each person and told them something personal that each would recognize as the truth. The scary part was when she said she was leaving her body now to journey to the next person's house. The people in the circle waited silently for about five minutes. Madam Bella began to speak again. She told the next man in the circle that there was a locked metal box under his bed and then she told him what was in it.

This day begins our adventure. Mother and I tread laboriously up the front walk after opening the front gate. I left the gate open, just in case we needed a quick emergency exit. Did I say that I am superstitious? Yes, well I believe in ghosts, too. OK, so I really did not want to be here. But here we were ringing the bell. Nothing. No response. I knocked, Mother knocked. My throat was pulsating with my heart. We were about to leave when a voice screeched out and it wasn't mine.

"Over here! Come 'round to the side!" a woman's voice crackled. My hand, groping for Mother's, felt clammy and cold as we approached the side of the house. Standing before us on the veranda was a wrinkled old woman, her long hair tied back in a scarf. Her slip, an inch longer than her mid-calf length dress and a tattered old sweater was her garb, or was this a costume? I smelled garlic as she reached out her hand for Mother.

"You have come to have your fortunes told. You are a half hour too late." Pointing to a gnarled old tree nearby she continued, "My sister hung herself this morning from that tree. I've cut her down and she is now inside. Please come in and wait with me for the coroner."

A small black cat brushed against my ankle, almost knocking me over. My eyes met Mothers. The blood had drained from her face. My feet became one with the sidewalk, and my cry for Jesus froze in my mouth before anyone could hear it.

Laughter. Her belly jiggled as tears fell from her quivering jowls. She was consumed in uproarious laughter.

"I am playing with you. The expressions on your faces are priceless! Come in."

Annette Martin Collins

The Apple That Saved Bea's life

Into the woods walked Patty and Bea
With a fine picnic lunch and mild tea.
Four deviled eggs, some bread and ham
Three apples, crackers, cheese and jam.

Behind the woods several fields lay
Bathed in the bright warm sun today
Spring is a lovely time of year
The song of the birds a joy to hear

Before they ate, Patty got up and ran
Chasing a butterfly, blue, gray and tan
Bea chose an apple, leaving the rest
To tuck in the pocket of her pretty dress.

A great mama bear from the brush appeared
Her two little cubs tumbled playfully near
Bea climbed a tree, what else could she do?
Then upon the same branch sat the tiny cubs, two.

Two tiny bears sat up in a tree
Up in the tree, two wee bears and Bea
Patty returned and saw Bea in the tree
With two tiny cubs, Oh my, oh me!

Patty spread the cloth quickly, upon it she lay
The fine picnic lunch Grandma made them today.
One apple was missing.
Bea had tucked it into the pocket of her dress.

"Toss the apple" Patty called. The cubs will follow.
"Humph… humph… Harumph", mother called angrily.
The cubs scrambled down as fast as they could
Chasing the apple Bea tossed towards the woods

Bea climbed down the tree and ran far away
The bears ate their fine picnic lunch today.
Guess what?
No berries, no pie! But grandma baked a gingerbread cake
and the girls had a good story to tell her.

Patty & Shelly, Friends Forever

Annette Martin Collins

The Anatomy of Me in February

Fingers… numb with cold while scraping frozen windshield
Feet… crunching cautiously across slippery parking lots
Face… bitten sharply by frigid winds whirling sand and snow
Ears… monitoring the crackle of blazing fire in the hearth
Eyes… wide with wonder as icy trees drip diamonds in the sun
Heart…lightened by the fun of choosing a valentine for someone
Soul… stirring with emotion at all these feelings
A gift from above…

A Haiku or Two

Sunset oft leaves
Castle Craig in silhouette
Before a mellon sky.

***

A silvery moon
slips across black satin sky
now studded with stars.

Peace

Could it be that this is Heaven?
Fresh air, mountains, beaches
Oceans, lakes, sunshine
Rain, flowers, green grass
Fruit, spices, vegetables
Trees, birds, animals

Could it be that THIS is heaven?

Search Ended

Where are you Lord…You great elusive external being
I have searched nigh half a century for a glimpse of you
As if obsessed…
In my naivety this search was for a miracle
My eyes wide in anticipation, I waited in expectation
And grew older…
My child rearing years a time of trial and tribulation
I called upon your name through tear-soaked pillow
Until I became calm and fell fast asleep
Where are you Lord…
You great elusive external being
I've searched mountains, valleys, cathedrals,
Throughout the north and south
Oft feeling Your presence…
Then directed inward my eyes finally saw Your Light
Burning softly in the window of my soul.
This was why You always answered when I called upon Your
name.
What affected me, affected You.
My discovery of Your omnipresence has given me new eyes
With which to see. Your hand has touched all matter
I look for you in the eyes of my neighbors
And wonder if they know….

The Frost Is on the Bumpkin

I think about aging daily. The anticipation of going to the State Fair in Raleigh had me both excited and apprehensive. Every year I go to the state fair by train with my friend Jeane, who owns a tour company. We leave her office and ride in a van to High Point, where we board a train, business class, directly to the state fair. Amtrak sets up a huge tent for its customers to rest after a day at the fair, to await the returning three o'clock train.

Remembering my experience of last year, I discussed concern with my daughters about attending this year. Last year, when trying to board the tram that circles the fairgrounds, I fell. The step was too high for me and my body hit the pavement like a sack of rocks. Getting up is never easy! Area gentlemen to the rescue.

A week before the day of the fair I was presented with a Rollator with a seat. Walking will be much easier and I can sit when I get tired. I bought Shelly a ticket this year so she was looking forward to a day at the fair also. Patty chose not to attend. Am I so old I now need a walker to assist me in things I use to take for granted, such as going to a fair? My grey hair gets whiter with every thought. Buck-up, buck-o! If the girls spent their hard-earned money on a Rollator for me, then by God, I am going to use it, embarrassed or not.

The day before the trip I got a phone call from my friend Jeane. She was in a panic because her driver backed out at the last minute. She talked to Shelly, to ask if she would consider driving the group to High Point. Shelly said yes, and since there were only five people going this year, Shelly would use her own car which holds seven people.

My Rollator, tucked into the trunk, one cane folded up in its seat, plus the cane I was using to assist me getting into the car, we were off to pick up the other passengers. It was only a matter of ten minutes at the train station before the train arrived. I left my old faithful cane in the car, and unfolded the back-up cane to keep with me on the train, for getting on and off. What a great ride it was in business class. There is more leg room, and we were offered coffee, tea, hot cocoa or water by a special conductor, just like on a plane with stewardesses. We left High Point at 8 A.M. and arrived in Raleigh at ten o'clock. Such a pleasant ride, and my thoughts were of eating a corn dog, fried dough, a sausage, pepper and onion grinder, and an ice cream.

I would not have enjoyed myself were it not for Shelly. She was at the ready lifting the Rollator over rocky, pebbly areas at the fair, and up and down stairs at certain exhibits. We occasionally found benches where Shelly and Jeane could rest and I sat on the Rollator seat. It was a pleasant day, even the weather held off on predicted rainstorms. It was not too cold, nor was it too hot.

I purchased three tickets to ride the tram and a handsome, curly haired, middle-aged man helped me on the tram. That was his job, to assist the elderly on and off the tram. It was senior day at the fair. I observed him as we rode around the fairgrounds assisting old women on and off the tram. He joked with each and every one. I felt crushed, knowing it was not only me who felt the flutter of butterflies in my heart. The attention of a handsome fella in a Harley Davidson T-Shirt caused me to feel twenty-one for a moment. I asked him how many proposals he had received already that day. He laughed and told me only three.

The conductor assisted with the folded Rollator, and several men offered their arms to help me off the train. I then decided that getting old is not such a bad thing, and I milked it the rest of the day! I saw many exhibits, and got ideas about things I could make by myself as gifts to give people at Christmas time. The final building we entered was near the exit gate. We each had an ice cream cone, a yearly tradition before leaving the fair.

While waiting for the train, Shelly and Jeane sat in the folding chairs under the big white tent, I on my Rollator. First ones to board were people going to Greensboro, then people going beyond that point, such as High Point. A special train came to pick us up. Shelly handed the Rollator up to the waiting attendant, and two other conductors hoisted my butt up onto the high step and into the train car. This car had plentiful leg room, and reclining seats. Guess what I did on the way home. Besides taking a nap, I thought about the corn dog and fried dough that I never got. I thought about the Italian sausage and pepper grinder I ate that was cold. The toasted coconut almond ice cream was delicious! The handsome man in the Harley Davidson T-Shirt who caused my heart to flutter for a moment or two. All the elderly gentlemen offering me their arms as I boarded and deboarded the train.

Like frost on a pumpkin my hair changed from dark to white in eighty autumns. Well, I am over being depressed about it. I have discovered that being old is not so bad. *This old bumpkin* can still have fun and work it when she wants to.

Maine

My love, I leave now, just
     As I came to you
Quietly
     Unannounced…
         Let me explain
Your beauty overpowered me
     I was alone
         Searching
            Fleeing
               Memories which caused pain
Like a philanthropist you
     Provided nourishment
         Guidance
            Encouragement
               Shelter from the rain
As teacher you nurtured me
     Illuminated my space
         Instilled
            Directed
               Swept shadows from my brain
Your raiment lush green forests
     Clear deep waters
         Cool
            Refreshing
               Without stain

I inhaled your aphrodisiac
     Of pine and mist of sea
         Yearning
            Learning
               My very soul aflame

But then, in echo of another time
     I heard the sounds of
         Necessity

Opportunity
    Sung in rhetorical refrain
My love, I leave now, quietly
    Just as I came, but filled with
        Peace
            Enlightenment
                For having known you, Maine.

Welcome to My World

Life Interrupted

Work, for me, was always interrupted by a need for respite. I never earned much money, giving my notice every few years at whatever job I had to seek help caring for my mother. Therefore, I was always "starting over".

This is a compilation of stories from the eighteen years of caring for my very much missed mother, and my mother-in-law. Both ladies were afflicted with Alzheimer's Disease. Both ladies had strength of character and were good natured. It is sad to see this disease progress and strip away memory day by day. At first it was little things like not being able to dress properly. Then, pouring orange juice into their coffee instead of cream. Things that we take for granted every day become a challenge to a person with this disease. The caretaker takes over at this point.

These stories are not to poke fun at this affliction. The stories are for sharing with other persons who must take on the responsibility as caretaker of a loved one. These are some of what I personally experienced. Remembering back, I can now laugh as some things were pretty funny and some things were frightening. I would give all that I have to be able to have these ladies back, to enjoy the years lost from the affliction that they had to endure. But they are both gone, and I hope and pray one day there will be a cure. It is so hard to see your loved one, knowing they don't recognize you at all. Every new day we start from scratch.

You are not alone. I know that living through the caretaker years will be hard and I hope you can find a caring support group to help you through it.

Houdini

Mother, Emily, came down with warning signs of Alzheimer's around the time of my divorce. I moved her in with me when I realized that she should not be living alone. At first, I left her alone in the apartment and went to work. But, one day, I came home and discovered a plastic cup melted into the stove top. She had tried to make a cup of coffee by putting water in a plastic cup and setting it on the stove to boil. Then she tried to put out the fire by using a dish towel. It was at that point I enrolled her into adult day-care. She did not want to go. She wanted to stay with me. She could not understand why she had to stay at 'that place' and it was so hard leaving her.

Emily was a good-looking woman for her age. She actually looked much younger that her seventy years, carried herself straight and poised. People would actually hold the adult day-care center door open for her and she would walk right out. She did not look like a client. On top of that, she was a walker. She walked a lot and could walk miles with no effort on her part. Each time she escaped from the day-care center I would get a call at work; would have to leave work to go out riding around looking for mother. After four escapes, Emily was expelled from the first center and admitted into another center. The second center lost her on three occasions. I was called each time. The last time, even the administrator went out searching for her. Guess who found her? I drove through the center of town where new construction was going on. This was seven miles from the place mother was being cared for.

There was Emily, the only person without a hard hat, standing in the middle of an excavation site behind chain link fencing. I took her home. She was glad to see me. I will never know if she walked all the way to town or someone gave her a lift.

Going Home to Mama

When Rose or Emily were feeling stressed or overwhelmed, they wanted to go home to Momma. One day, at Patty's house in Maine, Emily was feeling extremely agitated. I stood in the way of her going out the door. We kept the doors locked so she could not go outside by herself. She saw me as an obstacle and slapped me.

OK, I was not going to cause her any more stress, so I stepped aside after unlocking the door. Emily hurried out the door and walked down the long gravel driveway towards the unpaved road. The animals somehow knew that she was needing protection. Emily was first, several yards behind followed Sinbad, the malamute. He was followed by Sam, a Shepherd / Doberman mix, followed by Ezekiel, her seven-year old great grandson on his bicycle. Ezekiel was followed by his six-year old brother Levi, also on a bicycle. I brought up the rear. Oh, we were quite a parade! Emily was hot-footing it up the road (she was fast), the dogs were back and forth across the road enjoying every minute of this adventure. The boys were doing circles around everyone. I followed until Emily turned around and saw me.

She was happy to see me and by this time had forgotten where she was going. There was no traffic and no other houses nearby. We lived twenty miles from a town and surrounded by woods. She walked back towards me and we all went home.

One suggestion that I would like to offer you is when you are coping with a wanderer, label all clothing and put a note in the pocket of a sweater or other place with information that would be of use in identifying a person and where they live.

Rosie and the Christmas Slippers

Seven years after my father-in-law died, Rose met her old childhood sweetheart, Horace. They dated a while and he popped the question. She said yes. Rose moved into Harold's house in Orient, Maine. Rose was beginning to show signs of dementia but her granddaughter Patty kept a close eye on her grandmother. Every week Patty would go over to their house and clean the refrigerator of expired stuff. She would do some things around Rose's house and help her in any way she could.

Christmas Eve came, and Patty, Shelly and I all went to Rose and Horace's house to visit. They had one little dog, and one cat. Those were their children. As we sat around talking and watching television, having coffee and cookies Patty decided to have some fun with her grandmother.

Patty handed Rose a Christmas present and said it was OK to open one gift before Christmas. Rose was sitting on the couch with me and Shelly. She opened her box and there was a new pair of slippers. But these were not just any slippers. These were very special slippers. Rose took each slipper out one at a time and thought it was beautiful. They looked like cats. Two fluffy cats, black and white in color.

Rose took off her shoes and put on her new slippers. She was so proud of her new slippers. She had never had slippers that looked like cats before. She loved cats. Getting up from the couch, Rose began to walk around the room and somewhere in the house a cat began meowing. Rose looked here and there for the cat and called out "Here, Kitty, Kitty!"

She looked in the kitchen, no kitty. She looked in the bedroom, no kitty! She kept on calling the kitty and there was no kitty to be found. With every step that she took, a kitty would meow. She asked Horace if the kitty could be under the couch or in the cupboards. She wanted him to help her look for the kitty.

We all laughed until we couldn't laugh any more. Patty got Rose to sit down on the couch and removed her new slippers from her feet. She put Roses shoes back on and took the slippers out of sight. That night the slippers went home with Patty and she operated on them to remove the "meow" from the soles. Rose got her new slippers back the next day.

Rose Simpson Collins

The First Nursing Home

The adult day care in our town seemed unable to contain the likes of Emily. After many days and hours of interviews and evaluations for Emily, I was able to find a nursing home that I believed to be the best and got her approved for acceptance. My heart was broken leaving her there. I lied. I told her I would be right back when, in fact, I was planning my escape to home each night. I was there faithfully each night after work. I must confess, it was a relief not having to be up all night trying to get her back to bed. I was able to go to work each day well rested and then the evening visit would be an hour or two at the most. It was always hard leaving for home after our visits. She wanted to go with me.

One night after work I walked into the lobby of the nursing home and was met by a tall distinguished looking man in a wheelchair. "Say, would you give me a ride to the railroad station?" he asked. I replied I was there to visit my mother but if he had not found a ride by the time I was ready to leave I would give him one, since I drove past the railroad station.

There was Emily, sitting in a geriatric chair, parked at the nurses' station with several other residents. She was so happy to see me. I pulled up a folding chair and sat next to her. We held hands. Her verbal skills were deteriorating but we communicated with eye contact and holding hands. Occasionally I would catch her in a lucid moment and she could verbalize. I would ask, "Do you know who I am?". She would respond, my sister, or sometimes, my mother. The fact that I was her daughter had long been forgotten.

While holding hands, the gentleman in his wheelchair parked beside us.

"Do you have a cigarette?" he asked. I replied that I did not smoke. He then asked Emily, "Do you have a cigarette?". Emily looked at him with a stern expression then looked away. "Do you have a cigarette?" he asked again. I replied that she did not smoke either.

"Well, do you have a cookie?" he asked. This tugged at my heart. Emily was getting very agitated with him as he was getting more attention from me than she was, and all of a sudden, she yelled out "NO!"

Everyone looked at Emily. The sweet pesky man rolled away as fast as he could.

The next time I went to visit, Emily sat in the same spot near the nurses' station. The first thing I noticed as I entered was a puddle under her chair. Nurses were milling around the station but no one seemed to notice my mother. She was kept tied to prevent her from wandering at random. I knew that I would have to bring her home again. This was supposed to be one of the best nursing homes in the area. It was spacious and clean and lovely in appearance. The problem seems to be universal.

Homes are understaffed to create a higher profit. This was the first of several nursing homes that would share in the daily care of Emily.

Emily with a Doll, 1983

Call the Dentist

Emelie wore dentures. I remember Mother having beautiful teeth in her youth. She got a gum disease and had all her teeth pulled. During the six years that she was in the Maine Veteran's Home so many things happened. This story is just one of the things I want to remember.

Emelie had a roommate and her name was Edith. She was known to take things that did not belong to her. She was turned out of many a room that was not her own.

After Emelie lost her ability to converse more than a simple yes or no, and an occasional surprise word, she was the ideal roommate. She could tell no tales on anyone. Emelie never left her room without her soft brown teddy bear. His name was George. She named him George when she first got him.

One morning as the nursing staff was busy getting everybody washed and dressed for breakfast it was discovered that none of the residents had dentures in their bedside stand. Not one resident on that wing had dentures. A frantic search of every room began.

A major search of everyone's locker, drawers, windowsills, clothing, pocketbooks, trash cans. Wait... what's this? There is stuffing under Edith's bed. Where did it come from?

Then someone discovered George, Emelie's teddy bear. It had been unstuffed. Low and behold, several pair of teeth were inside George's tummy. Then inside a pillowcase in a closet in their room was a very large assortment of dentures.

The dentist had to be called. What a mess. Everyone had to be measured and refitted with their dentures. Each denture had to be engraved with an identifying mark so this would not happen again.

The big question was... WHO DONE IT? Emelie or Edith. Guess I will never know.

Thanks for the Memories

There are crocus now in blossom
Around the flagpole ring
Whose most delightful purpose
Being harbingers of spring.
Soon gone, but not forgotten
Followed by the daffodils
Then a multitude of colors
Softly waving from the hills.
Blue cornflowers and purple heather
Near our highways you may see.
Ah, yes, gone but not forgotten
Thank God for potpourri…

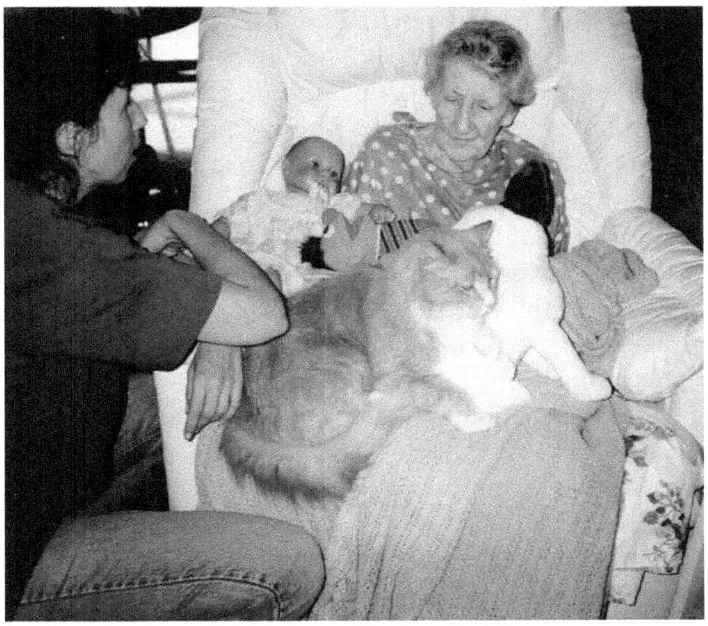

Shelly & Emily in Florida

Happy Birthday, Mom!

For your 77th birthday Shelly and I are taking you on a trip to Las Vegas for four days. I have the best, most caring daughters in the world.

The preparation for this trip and my overactive imagination ran amuck for two weeks until the night before we actually left for Charlotte. I stayed overnight at my daughters house the Saturday before we left as the plan was to leave at 3:30 a.m. Patty drove to Charlotte and our plane left at 7:00 a.m., to Chicago. I looked at a map and saw that Las Vegas was all the way across the country, next to California.

The next stage of the trip was flying from Chicago to Las Vegas. Since it was daytime, I got to see our beautiful earth from a heaven's view. There was what looked like crop circles in shades of red and brown, tan and grey. The next section of land was many rectangles cleanly cut out with what looked like one farm in the corner of each plot of land. Each plot was as large as a city from my observation seat. So far, my mission entailed the counting of everything. How much money I started out with ($200), how much things cost, how many crop circles I observed from the window of the plane, how many farms in uniform size, how often the stewardess came by to offer beverages, how many peanuts were in the little bag I bought in the terminal. Airlines do not offer free snacks anymore unless you want to purchase them at exorbitant prices.

The Rocky Mountains and the Grand Canyon took my breath away!

Our Earth is magnificent. Books and pictures do not do it justice.

There are 47 peanuts in a small bag of peanuts.

We got to Las Vegas and went to the MGM Grand. Patty had asked for a roll-away bed for our room. They said they did not have one so we had to upgrade to a suite for $150 more. Sunday afternoon, about four o'clock, we settled into our room and went down to the casino for a walk-a-bout. So many people! They come in all shapes, sizes and colors you know.

We saw the MGM Grand buffet and decided to have our evening meal there. Golden Coral in Winston Salem is about $11 per person on a Sunday. For the three of us to eat our dinner, the cost was $99 plus tax. The food was plentiful, but cold. There was a bottle of wine on the table as we were seated, but it was quickly whisked away as we did not want to pay extra for it.

HA! So much for the buffet and other fancy-schmancy restaurants. We found a food court in the building and that is where we ate for the rest of the stay. Yum…McDonalds, a pizza joint, and a chicken place.

Day two. The girls had gone out for coffee and a cigarette before I got up. I slept on the pull-out couch. I counted all the springs and rods in my mattress as I tried to find a comfy spot to settle into. I never said anything to the girls. I did not want them to switch places with me. They work 12 – 14-hour days, and I wanted them to have good rest. The girls brought me a cup of coffee and told me of their excursion. After getting up in the middle of the night they had gone to the casino and gambled a little bit, then sat and watched the hookers working their station. Yes, I said hookers. It is legal there. You can spot the working girls as they dress provocatively. My girls had a good time recalling what they saw. We went to McDonalds for breakfast, then walked back to the casino and I found the slot machine I wanted to play. It was a penny slot machine. You would think a penny machine was easy and cheap. Not so. The minimum bet on a penny slot machine is thirty cents. The girls left me there so they could walk around. I can't keep up with them anymore. An hour later they returned and found me sitting at the same slot machine with $800 in winnings. I cashed out at $621.00.

I gave Patty $600 to hold for me. The last time I gambled was in Atlantic City. This had been a bus trip from Connecticut. I went into the first casino with $300 in my pocket. Thirty minutes later I had enough left over to buy a hot dog on the boardwalk. I bought a hot dog, feeling really depressed. It was a good hot dog with mustard and sauerkraut. Standing at the railing, watching the water, suddenly a great big sea gull swooped down and grabbed my dog right out of my hands and flew away. The rest of the day I people-watched on the boardwalk until the bus came to pick us up. I can't be trusted at a casino.

Back to my Las Vegas story. I bought three tickets to ride the monorail for 24 hours. We rode to the end of the strip and visited three other casinos. Oh, so beautiful. Crystal and golden chandeliers, it was like being in heaven except for the flashing lights of the slot machines ringing and dinging.

Another night on the couch…ouch!

Day three. I got my morning cup of coffee delivered by my girls who returned from their morning coffee and smoke. We went to breakfast again at McDonalds. It is a long walk to the food court.

Back to the casino. I found a different machine to try. The girls left me for another walk-a-bout. Several hours later they returned to another surprise. I had $550.00 in winnings sitting in my machine. I cashed out at four hundred, then went right to the Kiosk selling tickets to *Circe-de-Soleil*, the performance of "Ka". The tickets were $240 for the three of us. My treat!

I also bought dinner that night. Yup…the food court.

The 7 p.m. show was the grandest performance I have ever seen in my life! I will never forget this awesome trip.

We were stuck in Dallas Wednesday night due to weather conditions. We stayed in a local hotel complements of the airlines. Sat in the airport in Dallas all day long…our flight was delayed again until 5 p.m. I snoozed in my seat. When I woke up, I was holding a coffee cup with 35-cents in it and a sign. MOTHER WITH TWO GIRLS STRANDED AT AIRPORT. PLEASE HELP.

PS: I RETURNED WITH $900 IN MY POCKET.

The EARL of Amity Maine

I met Earl when I was eighteen years old and newly married. He was my husband's uncle and quite a character. Uncle Earl lived in a camp he built in the woods of Amity. He was a hunter, fisherman, prankster, and the most beloved story-teller of the whole family of Simpsons. Earl was an alcoholic but everyone loved him in spite of his affliction. His stories got wilder and more outrageous as he partook of just another little sip of toddy. Earl never had children, but all the children in the Simpson family, and those that lived in the town of Amity were enamored by Uncle Earl.

The Mayor of Amity, well, that was a title he gave to himself. Everyone knew the mayor. As my children got older they always looked forward to a visit to Maine to see Uncle Earl. He would pile all the kids into the back of an old pick-up truck and off into the woods towards Jimmy Brook. Earl did not drink if he was around kids.

On one of his expeditions my kids came back with a story that Uncle Earl swore was true. One day Earl took a friend of his, who was visiting from Connecticut, into the woods to fish in Jimmy Brook. They were enjoying the silence of the forest, the babbling brook, a beer, when out stepped a man who asked to see their fishing license.

Uncle Earl took off like a shot into the woods and he ran and ran. Jumping over logs and brush and on and on, and just as quickly he stopped. Huffing and puffing, the warden caught up with him.

Here's my license, Earl said, still huffing and puffing.

"Why on earth did you run if you had a license on you?" the game warden asked.

"Well," said Earl, "The other guy didn't."

Annette Martin Collins

Remembering Mother in the Maine Veteran's Home

"Hi, Momma. How are you today?"

Every night after work I visit. Some nights I am her sister, other nights I am her mother. She has been here six years. Today you are 87. You have succeeded in winning over many hearts.

I love you.

I hear your soft shuffle as you come down the corridor, peeking into each room. Your smile brightens every corner of the room and there is no need to speak.

I love you.

Each face that you encounter reflects your cheery smile. Clutching your soft fat teddy bear you find a chair and sit a while.

I love you.

You named your teddy bear George when your mind was keener and you were still able to converse. Now the only words I hear is yes or no. But always that wonderful smile.

I love you.

We sit and hold hands. There is no need for speech. I feel her love through our hands. As I gaze at her she gently covers George with a blanket. I yearn for that flicker of recognition.

Every day I yearn, and I miss you.

Emily in Maine Veterans' Home

Faith

I dare to question you Lord.
You chose for me a mother who is gentle, sweet and kind.
In your great wisdom you arranged it so that she and I would
be living together. I thank You. All her life she worked hard
and dedicated her complete self to her family. Now I have a
chance to return a portion of the love that she showed me all
those years and what do You do? You send that thief
Alzheimer disease to live with us and steal away the one
possession that she kept for herself.
NO QUESTION GOES UNANSWERED
WHEN ASKED IN THOUGHTFUL PRAYER
Thank you, for now I know that every shred of memory that is
taken from her now shall be returned when she is no longer in
my care…
But in Yours.
I apologize.

Emily Martin

The Great Escape

The time for action was at hand. The girls and I had planned to take both my mother, Emelie, and mother-in-law Rose out of their individual nursing homes and move them to Florida with us. We already purchased a house in Melborne, Florida large enough to accommodate us all.

The first lady to be gathered up was my mother, Emelie. She was in the Maine Veterans Home in Caribou, Maine. On that day the weather was freezing cold. I had just washed my hair and went outside to the car from the motel. My hair froze into tinkling icicles. It was a sad good-bye to the staff at the Veterans home. They had been so good to my mother. They will probably remember her for a long time.

We then drove an hour and a half down country to Houlton, Maine. That is where Rose was living, in the Houlton Nursing Home. This was located just a half hour from her old homestead, in Amity, Maine. Rose knew everyone and everyone knew her. Being from a large family her brothers and sisters could visit her frequently. We gave this much thought. She was always such a large part of our lives that we did not want to leave her behind.

The plane trip was memorable. Emelie and Rose were seated in the first row of the plane with several pads on their seat just in case of accidents. We sat next to them. Emelie rarely spoke, while Rose was very verbal.

After looking around at her surroundings, Rose said to the stewardess, "Ain't this a nice big church!" The stewardess smiled at Rose and nodded in agreement.

Onwards to our new home and the beginnings of a new adventure.

Quick Witted Rosie

Once we got settled into our new home life became interesting. We girls all got jobs, different hours, so someone would always be in attendance for the ladies. Rosie could not walk, and she was sometimes verbally abusive. She liked to slap and bite.

One day, since Rosie seemed to be highly agitated, Patty handed her a doll and said, "Here, Grandma. Would you please watch the baby while I do the dishes?"

Rosie grumbled, "Do you think I have nothing better to do than to baby sit your kids for you?"

Patty & Rose

Living with Charles

Life, the good and the bad, is meant to be shared. I was married once. Even in bad situations there must be some good that comes out of it. My husband fixed my car when it broke down; he would jump start it in the cold weather so I could get to work. When we divorced after twenty-four years, I bought Triple-A Motor Club insurance. Triple-A does the same thing and they never yell when you need help.

My apartment, one year after divorce, consisted of five sunny rooms on the second floor of a three-family house. The kitchen was primarily white tile with white floor and appliances, yellow curtains. There was a double living-room off the kitchen divided by an archway.

A huge elephant-ear plant snaked its way along the archway giving the area a tropical look. The first living room, or den, had three large bay windows dressed with gold satin drapes. White and silver striped wallpaper brightened this room even on a cloudy day. The second living room, or parlor, had three sunny windows. A circular four-piece sectional of rose-burgundy had several small throw pillows scattered upon it. In the right-hand corner of this room there lived a ficus tree. In the summer I would decorate the tree with a few artificial birds. In the winter the tree was strung with twinkling white lights. Competing for the favorite focal point were an elephant-ear vine and an oversized umbrella plant that lived in the corner to the left. I loved all three plants, each no more or no less than the other.

There was a bedroom off to the right of the den, which was my room. Off to the right again, a bathroom, another bedroom, and back into the kitchen. It was a complete circle; kitchen, den, bedroom, bathroom, bedroom, kitchen. All the floors, with exception of the kitchen, were hardwood.

I had a good job. Each night I looked forward to going home to my quiet abode. But something was missing. The apartment was too big for one lonely person. I needed a cat. My first hurdle was asking the landlord.

Surprisingly, my landlord did not say no. I thought he might object since he was particular about cleanliness in his house. I assured him I would continue to keep the premises clean and tidy. His only other request was that the cat be declawed. I was on my way to the humane society before he closed the door to his apartment. My thoughts were of kittens playful and fuzzy.

A sign on both cages of kittens read, "Not available at this time." They had not been examined by the veterinarian. There were eight kittens in two cages. My heart sank, but I was there, so it couldn't hurt to look at the other cats. I walked the long isle of cages, two tiers on either side of the isle. Each cage housed a cat, sometimes two if they were small cats. There were cats of every color, long haired, short haired, some playful, some lethargic, a few were sleeping.

Do you believe in love at first sight? I do. It happened to me right there in that building. Last cage, top row left there lay an amber colored cat that seemed too large for his cage. His right front leg, dangling outside of the cage, beckoned me closer. My hazel eyes locked into the golden stare of this animal. I read the card on his cage: Two-year-old male, neutered, declawed, named Kitty. Kitty was too common a name for such a fine animal. He was mine. I was his. He did not object when I renamed him Charles Dickens. He became my new roommate that very night.

After a period of adjustment to his new home we became quite comfortable with each other. I am so grateful for having found Charles when I did at the humane society I often wonder why he was given up by his last owner. I have never been sorry that I chose Charles over a kitten. He loved the apartment as much as I did. He loved me. He would lay in the sun atop the curved sectional waiting for the birds in the ficus tree to fly off.

Every evening when I returned from work there was Charles, sitting in the window, waiting for me. When I had a problem and felt the need for a sympathetic ear I searched him out. We sat in the rocking chair and I stroked him until his purring brought me a sense of security. He was a good listener. We often communicated with our eyes, if you can believe that.

Charles was smart. One evening as I sat at the kitchen table he dropped a thick rubber band at my foot. His eyes were telling me to pick it up so I did. I picked up the rubber band and threw it into the living room. Charles bounded off into the living room after the rubber band and soon dropped it at my foot once again. He had taught me a game.

One evening, during an electrical storm, the power went off. I found my flashlight and shined it around the living room. Charles, at first startled by the light, began to chase the spot all around the floor, often sliding on his belly and bumping into objects. He had made up a game out of our dilemma, one we have played many times. He never tired of chasing the little spotlight zigzagging all over the floor. I tired of holding the flashlight after a while.

Charles had another favorite game. He taught me this one the first week he came to live with me. I was changing the sheets on the bed. I put the nice clean bottom sheet on and before the top sheet had landed Charles was on the bed, waiting. Charles became a lump under the sheet. He lay perfectly still. Sensing that this was to be another lesson, I patted the bed, calling "Where's the kitty?" I would pat here and then there, all the while saying, "Where's the kitty?" Charles would spring up to wherever my hand tapped. We would do this until one of us became tired of the game.

I really loved my cat. He has since gone to kitty heaven. I want to believe that there is such a place. I have moved several times since then, I now live with my two daughters. In memory of Charles, I feed feral cats. A few of them have pushed their way into my life and into my home. I love animals, I also love to write. Poets write of love. Here is my ode to Charles Dickens:

It's not just any cat who owns
A human such an me
We first became acquainted
At the humane society
I went to buy a kitten
But as I scanned each cage

A wistful, mature amber cat
Stole my heart with his gaze
He's never once regretted
The selection that he made
I hug him, pet and brush him
Then with treats he is paid
He's taught me to play hide-and-seek
And fetch the rubber band
Charles house-sits while I am at work
We share the day's demands
He truly is a dickens as
Before I tell him "SHOOO!"
He has jumped upon the table
Which was set for one…not two.
He slithers on his belly for
A little sniff of stew.
A kitty SWATT is what he gets
And his own kitty dish
Thank meew!

Charlie the Cat with Emily & Her Babies

The Luncheon

My mother-in-law, Rose, was not only a good cook, but a warm and personable hostess. She would go out of her way to put on a good meal when company came to visit. Rose remarried about seven years after losing her first husband. She lived happily with her new husband, a childhood sweetheart, until he could no longer care for her safely. Patty would go to Rose's house three times a week to clean out the refrigerator, and do simple household chores that Rose let slip. Now in her eighties, having many signs of Alzheimer's disease, Patty made the decision to bring Rose back home.

One night, Patty heard rustling and bustling in the kitchen. It was three a.m. Patty came to the kitchen to see Rose arranging a platter with everything from the refrigerator. All the vegetables were chopped up. There were carrots, celery, onions, tomatoes, cucumbers, plus eggs, cottage cheese, sliced cheese, cookies, crackers, cat crunchie's and dog biscuits.

Rose goes for a ride with Patty

Having a Baby at Eighty

My daughters and I were living in Florida, caring for my mother, Emelie, and also my mother-in-law, Rose. Emelie and I shared a bedroom. It once was a garage but remodeled into a fifth bedroom. Emelie had a hospital bed, while my bed was a twin. Rose had her own room which contained a hospital bed. Patty and Shelly each had their own room as well.

The kitchen/living room was large open area. Off the living room a door leading out to the sunroom then down two steps to a swimming pool. The ladies would sit out in that room in their wheel chairs watching pool. To ensure their safety the girls built a long bannister across the full length of the room so that the ladies could not roll themselves into the pool.

One day Rose and Emilie were sitting in their matching white recliners in the living room. Shelly and I were at work. Patty was home with the grandmothers. Both ladies were in their mid-eighties when we bought them life-like baby dolls. We discovered that when the ladies became agitated, we could hand them each a baby doll and they would become calm and quiet. It worked.

Emelie rarely communicated. She would nod, smile, frown, sometimes say yes or no, but she was a walker. Rose was extremely verbal, but she could not walk. Emelie had to be fed. Rose fed herself but her food mostly went to her stuffed dog without a nose. Once upon a time Rose and Emelie were friends, before the dementia. Now they were strangers.

Patty hears Rose yelling and she ran into the room to see what the matter was. Emelie was sitting in her chair holding her baby doll by one foot.

"That old HAG is going to drop the baby!" yelled Rose.

Patty takes the doll from Emelie and gives it to Rose. All was well in the world once again.

Annette Martin Collins

The Legacy

Great Spirit moves about the earth
And waves the tall field grass
He murmurs in the sparkling brook
And whispers through the pine and ash
Each living thing communicates
As sure as pristine water glistens
Please, before it is too late
Dear brothers, stop and listen.
Will there be lakes to swim or fish?
Will there be woods to hike?
Will there be unpolluted land
To plant a garden or the like?
Will there be cattle grazing here
Upon the vast flat plains
Or will they become extinct
Their grass destroyed by acid rain?
Will we see rolling ocean waves
Nudging tumbling shells to dry
Or will we see the oil-soaked birds
Flap and flutter, gasp and die?
What will our great grandchildren see
When they become as old as we?